D1488911

Beginning KARATE

Instructor Larry Brusacoram
and the following athletes
were photographed for this
book:
Chris Balus,
Jenny Cook,
Jerry Nguyen,
Katherine Trang Nguyen,
Amber Watroba,
R. J. Wilbur, and
Paul Yerich.

Beginning
KARATE

Julie Jensen
Adapted from Kim Dallas' *Fundamental Karate*
Photographs by Andy King

Lerner Publications Company
Minneapolis

Website address: www.lernerbooks.com

The Beginning Sports series was conceptualized by editor Julie Jensen, designed by graphic artist Michael Tacheny, and composed on a Macintosh computer by Robert Mauzy. The Beginning Sports series was designed in conjunction with the Fundamental Sports series to offer young athletes a basic understanding of various sports at two reading levels.

Library of Congress Cataloging-in-Publication Data

Jensen, Julie, 1957–
    Beginning karate / Julie Jensen ; adapted from Kim Dallas's Fundamental karate ; photographs by Andy King.
      p. cm. — (Beginning sports)
    Includes bibliographical references and index.
    Summary: An introduction to the history, skills, and techniques of karate.
    ISBN 0–8225–3512-2 (alk. paper)
    1. Karate—Juvenile literature. [1. Karate.] I. King, Andy, ill. II. Dallas, Kim. Fundamental karate. III. Title. I.V. Series.
GV1114.3.J465 1998
796.815'3—dc21   97–39121

Manufactured in the United States of America
1 2 3 4 5 6 – JR – 03 02 01 00 99 98

Photo Acknowledgments
Photographs are reproduced with the permission of: pp. 7, 8, © Dennis Cox/China Stock; p. 9, © ALL-SPORT USA/Doug Pensinger; p. 44, Courtesy of Jhoon Rhee, Fountain of Youth Foundation.

Contents

Chapter 1 . . . . . . How This Sport Got Started 7
Chapter 2 . . . . . Basics 11
Chapter 3 . . . . . The Moves 19
Chapter 4 . . . . . Self-Defense 35
Chapter 5 . . . . . Competition. 43
Chapter 6 . . . . . Razzle Dazzle 55
Karate Talk. 60
Further Reading 62
Index 63

How This Sport Got Started

Could you be as graceful as a ballet dancer and as tough as a boxer, at the same time? If you learn karate, you could be!

Karate students learn how to jump, kick, **punch,** and block. These moves help them get in shape, and help them protect themselves if they are attacked.

Karate is one kind of physical activity called martial arts. Some other martial arts are tae kwon do, aikido, judo, and kung fu. The martial arts were first practiced in Japan, China, Thailand, and Korea.

Once, only rich or royal people were allowed to have knives and swords. Poor people had to defend themselves with their bare hands—and their brains! Karate means "empty hand" in Japanese.

Murals and other artwork from ancient times show us how early athletes practiced and performed their martial arts. This mural is in the People's Republic of China.

7

Hundreds of years ago, Buddhist monks recognized the benefits of physical activity on mental and spiritual development. These statues of monks are in the Shaolin Temple in China.

A Japanese man named Gichin Funakoshi (foo-nah-KO-shee) is called the father of modern karate. He came up with a way to teach some basic movements to students. The students could use these moves to get in shape. They could also use the moves to fight off attackers.

When U.S. soldiers were in Asian countries during World War II and the Korean War, they saw people doing karate. The Americans wanted to learn how to fight that way.

Many karate schools in the United States teach students both the traditional and modern styles. Although some of the moves have changed, the basic rules of karate haven't. All forms of karate ask students for respect, control, discipline, and practice.

Karate once was used only to hurt another person. Modern athletes wanted to practice their sport without hurting anyone. That's how **sport karate** was developed. In sport karate, students can practice moves against an actual opponent without anyone getting hurt. Sport karate tournaments are for all levels of students. Athletes compete in controlled fights or do a **kata**.

The Many Faces of Martial Arts

Tae Kwon Do

Tae kwon do was first practiced in Korea. Although some people think Koreans started tae kwon do in the first century, it wasn't accepted as a martial art until 1955.

Jhoon Rhee brought tae kwon do to the United States in the 1960s. Tae kwon do is the most popular style taught in American martial arts schools.

Kung fu

Kung fu began in China. Students of kung fu use many foot and hand moves that were copied from animals. Many kung fu moves demand balance and strength.

Buddhist monks in China once carefully watched animals. They watched the animals hunt. They watched them feed. They watched them move quickly from place to place. Then, the monks began copying the animals' moves.

Some of the animals the monks watched were the praying mantis, white crane, tiger, and monkey. The monks named the moves after the animals.

Judo

Judo is another martial art that began in Japan. Judo students use many throwing and grappling techniques.

Jigaro Kano spent years studying jujitsu, another martial art. By 1882, he thought he had come up with a better method of fighting. He tried to use an attacker's weight against him or her.

Judo is an Olympic sport. In an Olympic match, contestants earn points for good technique. Putting an opponent on his or her back or holding them so they can't move for 30 seconds earns points.

Aikido

Morihei Uyeshiba discovered another way to defend himself. He moved his opponents into a circular motion and then locked their arms or legs at the joint. Uyeshiba found that he didn't have to be stronger than his opponent to do this. In 1926, he opened a school in Tokyo, Japan, and began training students.

His idea caught on. Many students have learned how to control an attacker with this method. Some American police officers use this style.

Chapter 2

BASICS

The first step in learning how to do karate moves is to find a school. Schools teach different styles of karate. Some schools teach mainly self-defense moves. Other schools teach traditional martial arts moves.

A school might focus on building students' self-confidence. Another school might give students many chances to **spar.** Try to choose a school in which you feel comfortable, with a teacher you like.

Karate is taught in a large room with mirrors on one wall. The students can watch themselves in the mirror to see if they are doing the moves correctly. The floor is wood or

Beginning with a Bow

*When all the students are ready to begin a class, they all bend at the waist and bow together. The **bow** is a sign of respect.*

In the photo above, Amber stands with her fingers together and her palms open. She holds her arms close to her sides. Amber's toes and heels are touching each other. She looks directly in front of herself. Amber's hands and arms stay still as she bows.

11

wood covered with carpet. Some rooms have a bar along one wall. Students use the bar to stretch or practice moves.

Before each class, the students line up in front of their instructor. When they are all silent, they bow.

Stretching

Karate students stretch their entire body before they begin practicing moves. Stretching out helps prevent injuries.

Stretching also helps students become more flexible.

The students begin by gently turning their heads in all directions. This helps stretch their neck muscles. Next, students put one leg in front of them and lean all their weight onto that front leg. They keep their back leg straight and touching the floor. This stretches the muscles on the tops of the thigh. Then, the students straighten out their front leg and bend over at the waist. This move stretches the muscles in the back of their legs.

Next, the students stand with their legs far apart. They bend at the waist and touch the floor. This stretches muscles in their legs and stomach.

The students then sit on the floor. They put their legs out in front of them and try to touch their chins to their knees. Then, they bring their feet together and in toward their body. This stretch, called the "butterfly," helps loosen the muscles in their hips. The students can also do this stretch with one leg out and one leg in, as Amber is doing in the photo below.

The students also do some stretches with partners. Jenny is helping Katherine stretch her legs in the photo at left. By stretching against some resistance, an athlete can become even more flexible.

Yelling

One of the very first things a karate student learns is how to yell. Does it seem silly to have to learn to yell? Most of us have been yelling for our whole lives.

A karate yell is different from a regular yell. A karate yell is quick and powerful. A karate yell is meant to scare an attacker. The best yell comes from deep within the lungs and windpipe. Squeeze your stomach muscles while yelling for a deeper sound.

Students also yell to get ready to defend themselves. A yell is part of taking a position to be ready to do a move.

Yelling has another purpose, too. Sometimes, students hold their breath when they are sparring or working on their moves. They are thinking so

hard about their actions that they forget to breathe. They have to breathe to yell, so yelling helps them to breathe properly.

Equipment

A karate student wears a top and pants called a **gi** (gee). A gi is usually made of cotton. It is lightweight and loose-fitting so students can do their moves

Some of the different colors of karate belts are shown below. Students try to move up to a higher belt level, as indicated by the color of the belt. To do so, they must pass tests given by their instructors. Some students wear lightweight karate shoes, shown in the bottom photo, but many students prefer to go barefoot.

comfortably. The uniforms come in many colors. Most students buy their gi from the karate school they attend.

Each student wears a cotton belt around his or her waist. The belt is tied in a square knot. The color of the belt indicates the student's level. To earn a belt, a student must pass a test for that level. In most schools, beginners wear white, gold, or yellow belts. Intermediate students wear green, blue, or purple belts. Senior students wear red or brown belts. The most advanced students wear black belts.

Class Time

After the class has started with a bow, the teacher will call out, "Ready." This tells the students to get into a certain position. Schools use different ready positions. Jenny is in a ready position in the photo at right. This ready position is called chunbi. Her feet are about shoulder width apart. She clenches her fists at her waist.

Karate classes can be small, even just one student. Karate classes can also be big, with as many as 20 students. Of course, a big class has to be in a big room so that students can do their moves without hitting other students.

Taking a karate class is the best way to learn karate. Your teacher and your classmates can help you learn how to do the moves safely. Don't try to teach yourself how to do karate moves. Use this book and other pictures as a guide for what you want to learn. Then, find a karate school that you like, make sure it has plenty of pads, and get busy!

Chapter 3

THE MOVES

There are two types of karate—classical and practical. Classical moves are traditional martial arts moves. Classical moves are used in katas. A kata is a series of moves performed against an imaginary opponent. Practical moves are classical moves that have been changed a little to be more practical for self-defense.

On the following pages, you will see karate students doing many different moves. You can learn a lot just by looking at the pictures. If you want to learn how to do some of the moves you see in this book, take a karate class. The teacher will be sure that you learn to do the moves correctly. You will also have a safe, padded area in which to learn. Plus, you'll have other students to help you practice.

In a classical move, the student's feet stay flat on the floor, as in the photograph above. In a practical move, the student's heel may leave the floor, as demonstrated in the photo below.

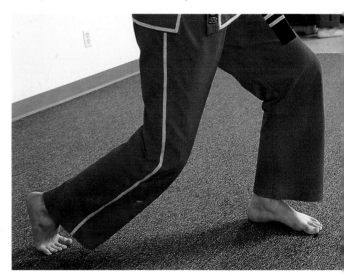

Fighting Stance

First, a karate student learns a correct **stance.** A stance is the position a student takes to begin any move.

Paul is in a practical fighting stance at left. He stands sideways to his attacker. His front fist protects his face. His other fist is close to his body. Paul's knees are slightly bent and his legs are apart.

Hand Strikes

Some hand strikes are quick, like the **backfist** and the **jab.** Other hand strikes are meant to be powerful, like the punch, **hammerfist,** and **palm heel.** A student must learn how to use his or her entire body while doing a hand strike.

● *Punch*

The student begins by curling the punching hand into a tight fist. Keep your thumb outside your other fingers. Some beginners tuck their thumb inside the fist. This is a mistake. They could break their

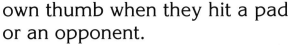

own thumb when they hit a pad or an opponent.

In the top two photos, Chris shows how to do a practical punch. He starts with his fists close to his body. Then he leans forward and thrusts out his punching hand, straight ahead of himself. His heel lifts off the ground as he drives his body forward for the most power.

R. J. is doing a classical punch in the photo at right. He throws the punch while keeping both feet flat on the ground.

● *Jab*

The jab is a quick hit to an attacker's face. Katherine starts with her feet apart and her weight centered. Her fists are tightly closed.

Katherine shoots out her front hand straight in front of herself. She lunges toward her attacker. She uses her two largest knuckles to hit her opponent.

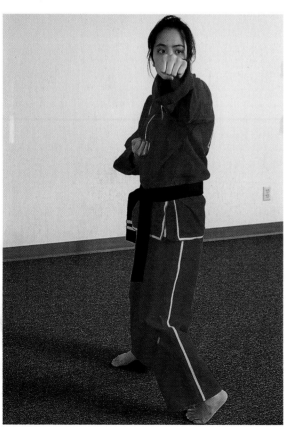

● *Hammerfist*

To throw a hammerfist, Jerry starts in the same stance as he would to throw a punch. Then, Jerry lifts his striking hand up above his head. He quickly swings down his hand, striking his opponent's nose with the bottom of his fist.

Jerry's front hand hardly moves during the hammerfist. He keeps his non-striking fist close to his face.

● *Palm Heel*

Jenny stands as if she's ready to throw a punch. The palm of her striking hand is open with her fingers and thumb curled tightly toward her palm.

Jenny drives her hips forward as if she were throwing a punch. Her wrist is pulled back. She drives the heel of her palm right below the attacker's nose. After the hit, Jenny opens her fingers and rakes them across the opponent's face.

Kicks

Karate has a variety of powerful kicks. Some kicks are used for self-defense. Others are used mainly in competition.

To do an effective kick, a karate student needs power, flexibility, correct positioning, and speed. A karate student can hit a person from farther away with a kick than with a hand strike. Most students also kick with more power.

● *Round Kick*

A **round kick** is a quick kick. Students use round kicks to score points quickly in sparring matches. Round kicks are often aimed at the opponent's head, stomach, or chest.

In the photos at right, Jenny does a good round kick. She first turns her hip. Then she pulls her knee waist high and back. Jenny snaps out her lower leg and strikes her opponent with the top of her foot. She keeps her hands close to her body for protection. After she kicks her opponent, she snaps her leg back and away from him or her.

● *Side Kick*

A **side kick** is one of the most powerful kicks in karate. When done correctly, a side kick can stop an attacker.

Chris first brings his kicking leg up and turns his hip. Then he snaps out his leg. As he hits his attacker, Chris locks his knee so that the full force of his extended leg slams into the other person. After snapping out his leg, Chris quickly brings his leg back to his body so his attacker cannot grab it.

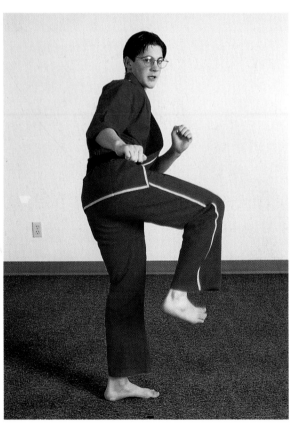

● *Side Stomp*

A **side stomp** can be used on the knee or ankle of an attacker. Amber does a side stomp in these photos.

Amber pulls her knee back and up to her waist. Then she extends her leg and locks her knee as she strikes the target.

● *Front Kick*

The **front kick** is another powerful kick. It is often aimed at an attacker's head, chest, or groin. R. J. shows a front kick in the photos above.

R. J. first lifts his front knee straight up and waist high. He points his foot down, but curls his toes backward. R. J. whips out his leg and strikes his target with the ball of his foot. That way, he won't break his toes when he hits the target.

R. J. keeps his hands and arms up while he does the front kick. After he hits his target, he quickly snaps his foot back to his body.

● *Thrust Kick*

The thrust kick is a type of front kick. Katherine is doing a thrust kick into a pad in the photos on this page.

Katherine first pulls her knee up and into her chest. Then, she thrusts her leg and all of her weight completely forward and into the target.

Blocks

Knowing how to block an attacker's strikes is as important as knowing how to strike an attacker. The **high block**, **forearm block**, and **low block** are the most common blocks. In these blocks, students use their forearm to block the blow.

● *High Block*

The high block is very effective against attacks to the head and face. Jerry demonstrates this block in the photos on this page.

First, he crosses his forearms in front of his body. Then, he snaps his top arm over his head.

Jerry makes sure he does not have his blocking arm in front of his face or directly above his head. If he did, his attacker could slam Jerry's blocking arm back into Jerry's body.

Jerry keeps his non-blocking hand against his chest, ready to strike. He stays in his stance, with his knees slightly bent for support and balance, during the block.

● *Forearm Block*

Use the forearm block against strikes to the chest and face. Amber shows the correct form for an inside forearm block in the photos on this page.

Amber starts in a regular stance. Then she brings her forearms across her body and thrusts out her blocking forearm to block the strike. Amber's blocking arm stays bent throughout the block. Her non-blocking hand stays close to her body to protect her.

● *Low Block*

Students use the low block mainly against kicks to the groin and stomach. To do a low block, Paul first raises his blocking hand up by his ear. He keeps his arm close to his body. Then Paul snaps out his fist toward the kicker. At the same time, he shifts his front foot over slightly for balance. He bends his front knee, which forces his weight forward. Paul keeps his non-blocking hand close to his body, in case he needs to throw a hand strike at his opponent.

Chapter 4

SELF-DEFENSE

Karate students know that it is better to avoid a fight than to get into one. If someone is threatening you, first talk with your teachers or parents. Perhaps talking with the person will stop the threats. But if that does not work, remember that no one has the right to hurt you. You can protect yourself. Learning some self-defense strategies can help you if you are attacked.

Don't try these moves until you have learned them from a qualified teacher. There are many ways to defend yourself. The key to doing any of these moves is to practice them over and over again with proper coaching and equipment. With practice, your moves will become quick and sure.

Tools for Training

Many students use heavy body shields, or pads, when they are learning to do powerful kicks. A partner holds the pad. When the teacher gives the command, the student kicks the pad. The padding allows the student to kick as hard as he or she can without hurting the partner.

Some students use old X-ray papers to practice their aim. Above, Katherine is working on keeping her knee level in a round kick. She is concentrating on doing the kick correctly and hitting her target on the paper, rather than putting a lot of force into the kick.

A heavy bag can be used without a partner. Students can hit the bag as hard and as often as they want. Sometimes students take turns seeing who can move the heavy bag the furthest with one kick or punch.

Choke Hold

If someone grabs your neck in a choke hold, remember that your arms and legs are still free. The attacker's wrists are the weak link.

Katherine shows how to get out of a choke hold in the photos on this page. She grabs her attacker's arm with her left hand. She reaches back with her right fist. Then she quickly twists her body while hitting her attacker's wrists to break the hold.

Wrist Grab

If you pull away from a wrist grab, the attacker will just squeeze tighter. In the photos on this page, Jerry disables his attacker without escaping from the hold.

Jerry raises his knee to his waist and stomps the attacker's knee. The attacker continues to hold on so Jerry throws a hammerfist to his face.

To escape a wrist grab, twist through the attacker's thumb. Pull up and through the person's thumb and index finger.

Shoulder Grab

An attacker may grab your shoulder or the front of your shirt. If this happens, remember that both your arms and legs are free.

In the photos on this page, Chris shows how to escape quickly. He steps back with the foot opposite the shoulder that is being grabbed. The attacker has grabbed Chris' left shoulder so Chris steps back with his right leg. Chris then throws a high block as close to the attacker's wrist as possible. Chris follows the escape with a front kick to the groin.

Grab from Behind

Being grabbed from behind is scary. Amber demonstrates how you can escape from this attack.

Amber raises her left arm and steps behind and toward her attacker with her left leg. She then twists her body to break the hold. She throws a palm heel into the attacker's face.

Bear Hug

In the photos on this page, Katherine shows one way to get away from a bear hug. She side stomps her attacker's ankle. That forces him to loosen his grip. Katherine then steps to one side of the attacker and strikes his groin with a hammerfist.

Hammerlock

Jenny's attacker has cranked back her right arm and grabbed her left shoulder. Jenny knows at least one way of getting out of this hammerlock.

First, she steps back with her left leg. Then, Jenny lifts her left arm and points her elbow straight out in front of her. Next, she twists around, dropping her left arm across the attacker's body. This breaks the hold. Then Jenny pulls back her left arm and thrusts it toward the attacker's jaw.

Remember, don't try any of these moves without a teacher and safety equipment. These moves can be dangerous. And always remember, avoiding a fight is better than winning one.

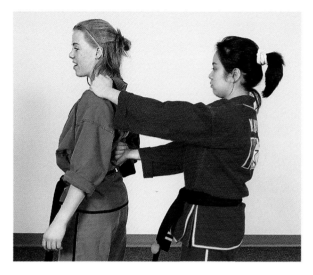

Chapter 5

COMPETITION

If a karate student was attacked, that student probably would feel nervous and afraid. Fear might make the student forget what he or she had learned. Some karate teachers think that learning to deal with fear is an important part of training. Tournaments give students a chance to test their skill and nerve.

Most tournaments have two parts—katas and sparring. Students are grouped by belt rank, age, size, and sex so that the competition is fair.

When a student enters a tournament, the student's school, age, rank, and size are recorded. The student pays an entry fee and is assigned a ring number and event time. Many students study other competitors before it's their turn.

This karate student is competing in the weapons kata division. Weapons used in competition are not sharpened.

43

Tae Kwon Do Master

Jhoon Rhee introduced many Americans to karate with his spectacular board-breaking shows in the 1960s. Rhee began by demonstrating his moves at colleges across the United States. As his popularity grew, so did his list of interested students. Even movie star Bruce Lee learned kicks from Rhee.

The Jhoon Rhee System focuses on body positions that increase the power and speed of moves. Rhee also began using pads during sparring matches. Many karate students had been injured while sparring. The injured students had to stop training until they healed. Rhee made padding that was easy to use. Padding is used in sport karate tournaments all over the country.

Kata

A kata, or series of karate moves, gives a student the chance to demonstrate speed, skill, intensity, and precision. A kata is like a gymnast's routine. It has certain moves that must be done in a specific order.

Karate students start with katas that are designed for beginners. A beginner may only have to do punches and blocks. A beginner's kata may have just two times when the student has to change direction. More advanced students do katas with jumps, spins, punches, and blocks. They may have to change direction eight times in a single kata.

Some katas show off a student's power. Others require speed and flexibility. Some katas are as old as the sport itself. Others were created by black belt masters. Some schools even let black belt students make up their own katas.

There are several types of katas. Students often compete in more than one category.

● Musical

In musical katas, the karate student must match each move to the correct music, much like a gymnast does in a floor exercise routine.

● Asian

Asian katas are traditional. They are not done to music, and do not include any non-traditional martial art moves.

● Weapons

Competitors in this kata division use a **bo,** machete-like knives, or a three-pronged **sai.** The weapons are not sharp.

● American

In this category, students do any of the many katas their schools have developed. Some students do gymnastics moves, such as flips, with karate moves.

In the photos below and on the next two pages, Amber does some of the moves in a beginner's kata.

● *Judging*

To begin a kata competition, the student steps into a ring. The student tells the judges his or her name, school, and the name of the kata. This can be a scary moment for the student. Some students have even for-gotten their own names during the introduction! Luckily, the judges did not take away any points for that.

The student bows to the judges and then does the kata. The judges are experienced black belts. They judge the stu-dent on how perfectly he or she

Traditional katas were developed by the ancient masters to instruct and to test students.

does the moves. The judges also look for how intensely the student concentrates. Katas were first created by the old masters to give students a chance to practice fighting against imaginary opponents. The judges want the student to do the moves so convincingly that the judge can almost see the student's attacker.

The judges give each student a score from a low 7.0 to the highest score of 10.0 points. After all the students have performed, the judges announce the first, second, and third place winners.

Amber does punches and blocks as part of her kata. Jumps and kicks are included in other katas.

Katherine's smile shows off her clear mouth-guard. In addition to a mouthguard, students wear protective padding on their heads, hands, and midsections when they spar.

Sparring

Karate students put all their moves together against an actual opponent when they spar. For many students, sparring is the most fun part of karate.

Any fighting, even practice fighting, can be dangerous. Most teachers only allow advanced students to spar. Practice fighting helps students learn quick reactions. Sparring practice also builds the students' confidence in a safe setting. Everyone who spars wears pads to prevent injuries.

Teachers help students learn timing and strategy for sparring. Strategy might include how to set up a hand or foot strike. Students might spar for two to three minutes during each class while the teacher watches. The sparring sessions are short, but they can be tiring. Most students feel afraid when someone attacks them. Beginners often throw wild punches or freeze up and do nothing. These approaches wear down a student. As students practice, they begin to

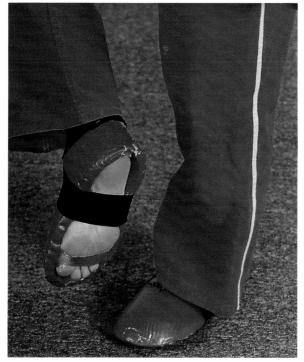

Above, Jenny and Katherine practice their moves during a sparring session. At left, students wear protective pads on their feet while sparring.

relax during a sparring match. They learn to save energy and throw only the best moves.

Students also learn how to avoid being hit while sparring. This may sound easier than it is. Good karate fighters know how to set up moves so their opponent does not see what is coming. Karate students have to learn how to use their power, speed, and wits.

● *Point Sparring*

To start a match, the center judge or timekeeper calls the two students into a ring. The students stand opposite each other and bow. The center judge holds his or her hand between the two contestants. To start the two-minute match, the center judge raises his or her arm while saying, "Fight."

The sparring judges are black belts. As strikes are thrown, three judges decide whether points should be given for each strike. To earn a point, two of the judges must agree that the strike was clean and that it hit a legal target area with controlled contact. Each fighter may earn up to five points.

In most cases, punches thrown to the body or head are worth one point. Kicks are worth two points. Each punch or kick must strike the target clearly and cleanly.

The head, face, chest, ribs, abdomen, and kidneys are legal targets. The groin, knees, ankles, back, and neck are not.

If a fighter does an illegal move during the match, the judges would warn him or her. If the fighter did it a second time, the fighter's opponent would be given a point. If the fighter did a third illegal move, the fighter would be disqualified.

In the photos at right, R. J. and Chris are sparring. The photos show them doing punches and kicks that they might use in a match.

Chapter 6

RAZZLE DAZZLE

Karate movies and television shows dazzle viewers. How can those action heroes do those amazing things? Remember, camera angles, lights, and special effects can make anyone look spectacular. A real karate master doesn't need any help to impress an audience.

Black belt students practice for years to develop incredible speed and flexibility in moves. In the photo on this page, Jerry shows off a jump spin wheel kick. He needs awesome speed and control to do this move.

When Jerry began learning this move, he jumped and spun without doing the kick. As he got stronger, he added the kick. Then, Jerry spent hours practicing in front of the mirror to develop a balanced spin and kick.

Special moves, created just for tournaments, are called exhibition moves.

Below, Jerry, Chris, and Jenny do a perfectly timed jump split kick.

Fans love to see karate masters break boards. Many black belts side kick a board. Others like to punch the board.

Paul is using an elbow strike to break the board in the photo above. First, Paul and R. J. put the board at the right height for Paul. Paul focuses on his target. He lines up his body and his elbow. Then Paul shifts his weight forward. He thrusts his elbow through the board, yelling as he breaks it.

Karate students need to be flexible. In the photo above, Jenny shows how flexible she is. Her legs are straight up and down. Jenny has stretched before and after her workouts to become so flexible. At the left, Chris shows how he uses his flexibility in a side kick.

Here, R. J. does a dazzling
tornado kick, showing balance
and control. He spins around in
a circle and keeps his body
almost straight up and down
when he kicks.

All of these karate moves
take lots of practice. And the
rewards of studying karate go
far beyond doing dynamite
kicks or facing up to bullies.
Karate is a fun and exciting
sport for any athlete!

KARATE TALK

backfist: A punch thrown by swinging the forearm away from the body with the palm facing inward. The target is hit with the back of the fist.

bo: A long, rounded wooden stick used in a weapons kata.

bow: A move done by bending forward at the waist. A bow is a traditional sign of respect between students and instructor, and between sparring partners.

forearm block: A defensive move in which the karate student sweeps a forearm in front of his or her body to block attacks to the chest or face.

front kick: A defensive move in which the karate student extends a leg directly in front of him- or herself. The student uses the ball of the foot to strike an opponent.

gi: The standard karate uniform of a loose-fitting top and wide-legged pants. The uniform is closed with a belt, the color of which indicates the student's ability.

hammerfist: A strike performed with a tightly closed fist used with a powerful sweeping motion.

high block: A defensive move in which the karate student uses a forearm raised above the head to block attacks to the face and head.

Paul, Jenny, and Jerry are each using a bo in this weapons kata.

jab: A quick, tight-fisted punch that is delivered straight on.

kata: A series of traditional martial arts moves that are done in a specific sequence or routine.

low block: A defensive move in which the karate student uses a forearm to block attacks to the groin and stomach.

outside block: A defensive move in which the karate student uses a forearm to push away any attacks to the chest or face.

palm heel: A punch that is delivered with the fingers curled tightly down and the palm facing outward to strike the target.

punch: A strike that is delivered with a tight fist. The hand is held close to the body before the student strikes the target with the two largest knuckles first.

round kick: A fast kick in which the karate student uses a snapping motion and strikes the target with the top of the foot.

sai: A three-pronged weapon that is used in a weapons kata.

side kick: A powerful kick in which the karate student extends a locked leg and strikes an opponent in his or her chest or face with the heel of the extended leg.

side stomp: A move in which the karate student extends a leg sideward and downward to strike an opponent's knee or ankle.

spar: A form of controlled fighting in which two karate students wearing protective gear use punches, kicks, jabs, and blocks to strike each other. Competitive sparring is done on a 26-foot square mat.

sport karate: A form of competitive karate in which karate students use their moves against actual opponents without harming them.

stance: A position the karate student takes before beginning a move.

Chris, R. J., and Katherine demonstrate side kicks of various heights.

FURTHER READING

Blot, Pierre. *Karate for Beginners*. New York: Sterling, 1996.

Corcoran, John. *The Martial Arts Sourcebook*. New York: Harper Perennial, 1994.

Goedecke, Christopher. *Smart Moves*. New York: Simon and Schuster, 1995.

Metil, Luana and Jace Townsend. *The Story of Karate*. Minneapolis: Lerner Publications, 1995.

Mitchell, David. *The Young Martial Arts Enthusiast*. New York: DK Publishing, Inc., 1997.

Morris, Ann. *Karate Boy*. New York: Dutton, 1996.

Queen, J. Allen. *Complete Karate*. New York: Sterling, 1993.

Queen, J. Allen. *Karate Basics*. Minneapolis: Lerner Publications, 1992.

FOR MORE INFORMATION

Aikido Association of America
1016 W. Belmont
Chicago, IL 60657

All American Taekwon-do Federation
P. O. Box 9430
Wilmington, DE 19809

American Ju-Jitsu Association
P. O. Box 1357
Burbank, CA 91507

American Karate Association
P. O. Box 214
Momence, IL 60954

American Karate Federation
250 New Litchfield St.
Torrington, CT 06790

American Kenpo Karate Association
6469 S. W. 8th St.
Miami, FL 33144

American Taekwon-do Association
6210 Baseline Road
Little Rock, AR 72209

International Ninja Society
P. O. Box 1221
Dublin, OH 43017

National Women's Martial Arts
 Federation
5680 San Pablo Ave.
Oakland, CA 94608

North American Amateur Contact
 Karate/Kickboxing Association
255 S. W. Higgins
Missoula, MT 59803

United States Judo Federation
19 North Union Blvd.
Colorado Springs, CO 80909

United States Karate Association
P. O. Box 17135
Phoenix, AZ 85011

United States Taekwondo Association
220 E. 86th St.
New York, NY 10028

INDEX

aikido, 7, 9

belts, 16, 43, 44, 55–59
blocks, 31–33; forearm block, 32; high block, 31, 38; low block, 33
board-breaking, 44, 57
bowing, 11, 12, 46
breathing, 15

chunbi, 17
class, 11, 17, 19
classical martial arts, 19, 21
competition, 8, 43–44. *See also* kata; sparring

equipment, 16–17, 35

fighting. *See* sparring
fighting stance, 20
fighting styles, 7–9
flexibility, 13, 14, 25, 58
Funakoshi, Gichin, 8

gi, 15–16

hand strikes, 20–24; elbow strike, 57; hammerfist, 23, 37, 40, 41; jab, 22; palm heel, 24, 39, 41; punch, 19, 20–21, 41, 57
history of martial arts, 7–9

judo, 7, 9
jujitsu, 9

Kano, Jigaro, 9
kata, 8, 44–47; American, 45; Asian,

45; judging, 46–47; musical, 45; weapons, 45
kicks, 7, 25–30; front kick, 29, 38, 41; jump spin wheel kick, 55; jump split kick, 56; round kick, 25; side kick, 26–27, 44, 57, 58; side stomp, 28, 36, 40, 41; thrust kick, 30; tornado kick, 59
kung fu, 7, 9

Olympic Games, 9

practical moves, 19, 21

ready position, 17
Rhee, Jhoon, 9, 44
routines. *See* kata

schools, 11–12, 17, 44
self-defense, 11, 19, 35; bear hug, 40;
    choke hold, 36; grab from behind,
    39; hammerlock, 41; shoulder grab,
    38; wrist grab, 37
sparring, 48–53; point sparring, 50–53
sport karate, 8, 43–53
stretching. *See* warmup
styles of karate, 7, 8, 9. *See also*
    classical martial arts; traditional
    martial arts

tae kwon do, 7, 9, 44
tournaments. *See* competition
traditional martial arts, 7, 8, 11, 19, 45
training aids, 35

Uyeshiba, Morihei, 9

warmup, 12–14

yelling, 14–15, 57

Amesbury Public Library
149 Main Street
Amesbury, MA 01913